Oracle DBA Checklists

Pocket Reference

RevealNet

Beijing • Cambridge • Farnham • Köln • Paris • Sebastopol • Taipei • Tokyo

Oracle DBA Checklists Pocket Reference

RevealNet

Published by O'Reilly & Associates, Inc., 101 Morris Street, Sebastopol, CA 95472.

Editors: Deborah Russell and Jonathan Gennick

RevealNet Editor: Steve Hilker

Production Editor: Rachel Wheeler

Cover Designer: Ellie Volckhausen

Printing History:

April 2001: First Edition.

0-596-00122-3
[C]

Table of Contents

Oracle DBA Checklists Pocket Reference

Introduction

The purpose of the *Oracle DBA Checklists Pocket Reference* is to help Oracle DBAs quickly look up the procedures they'll need to follow when performing key Oracle database administration tasks.

This book is divided into three major sections covering the three main areas of an Oracle DBA's responsibilities: database management, installation and configuration, and network management. While we can't possibly cover every DBA task in this concise reference, we've highlighted the most important tasks within each of these three fundamental areas. The information presented here should be helpful to both new and experienced DBAs.

Each section takes a "cookbook" or checklist-style approach to presenting the material. Our goal is to make the most important DBA information as accessible as it can be so you'll be able to use it most effectively in your daily work. While we've designed the steps to be easy to follow, please note that this book is not a self-contained user guide; basic knowledge of Oracle, SQL, and SQL*Plus is assumed. You will need to refer to Oracle documentation and other third-party books for detailed information. In addition, every Oracle site has its own special procedures. You'll need to supplement the procedures described in this book and in the Oracle documentation with your own site's procedures.

Conventions

The following typographical conventions are used in this book:

Italic
: Used for filenames, directory names, and URLs

`Constant width`
: Used for code examples and the output of commands

`Constant width italic`
: Indicates that the item (e.g., a filename) is to be replaced by a user-specified value

`Constant width bold`
: Indicates user input in code examples

UPPERCASE
: In syntax descriptions, usually indicates keywords

lowercase
: In syntax descriptions, usually indicates user-defined items such as variables

[ ] In syntax descriptions, enclose optional items

NOTE

Before Oracle8*i*, Oracle commands were typically issued from Server Manager (*srvmgrl*). Starting with Oracle8*i*, Oracle recommends that you issue commands from SQL*Plus. In most cases, however, issuing these commands from Server Manager will still work.

Acknowledgments

The information contained in this pocket reference is extracted from the *RevealNet Knowledge Base for Oracle Administration*. Special thanks go to the following Knowledge Base authors whose expertise was used in the development of this book:

Michael R. Ault is an OCP-certified Oracle7, Oracle8, and Oracle8*i* DBA with over 15 years of experience. He has participated in the Oracle8 and Oracle8*i* beta programs. Mike is the author of *Oracle8i Administration and Management* (John Wiley & Sons) as well as several other Oracle books and numerous articles on Oracle. He is a partner in The DBAGroup LLC, a consulting firm providing DBA and training services on Oracle projects. He is also the Sysop for the RevealNet DBA Pipeline (*http://www.revealnet.com*). He is a frequent contributor to *DBMS*, *Oracle*, *DBPD*, and other magazines, as well as a frequent presenter at Oracle Open World, IOUG-A, and ECO.

Thomas B. Cox is a former Oracle employee and author of the *Oracle Workgroup Server Handbook* (Oracle Press), as well as the *Low Administration Oracle Specification*, the *Oracle DBA Checklist*, the *DBA Maturity Model*, and many other white papers and articles. He now works for PricewaterhouseCoopers.

Jonathan Gennick is an Oracle Certified Professional and writer. Jonathan has written or coauthored a number of Oracle books, including *Oracle SQL*Plus: The Definitive Guide* (O'Reilly), *Oracle Net8 Configuration and Troubleshooting* (O'Reilly), and *Oracle SQL*Loader: The Definitive Guide* (O'Reilly). He recently joined O'Reilly as an associate editor specializing in Oracle books.

Jim Lopatosky is an Information Technology Consultant for the Maine State Government's Bureau of Information Services (Augusta, ME), specializing in Oracle database administration. Jim has been involved actively with Oracle User Groups. He took office as President of the Northeast Oracle Users Group (NOUG) in October of 1999. Previously he founded, and presided for three years over, Maine's Oracle Users Group (MSOUG).

Hugo Toledo is Director of Engineering at DaVinci Software in Chicago. Hugo has worked extensively with

Oracle's connectivity technologies since 1989 and is a frequent speaker at industry conferences. His latest book is *Oracle Net8 Configuration and Troubleshooting,* written with Jonathan Gennick (O'Reilly).

We would also like to thank our reviewers:

Stephen Andert reviewed the Net8 section of this book. He is a DBA for First Health Group Corporation and has 10 years of experience working with database technologies. Stephen's Net8 expertise contributed greatly to the accuracy and relevance of the Net8 material in this book.

Victor Slootsky is a Senior Oracle DBA at BAE Systems in Rockville, MD. He is an OCP-certified Oracle7, Oracle8, and Oracle8*i* DBA with over 20 years of IT experience. Victor is a member of the faculty of the Johns Hopkins University (JHU) and founder of an Oracle educational environment at the Montgomery County Campus of JHU. There, he has authored and coauthored a number of educational materials about Oracle database administration. He also has authored 11 publications in various scientific journals.

Database Management

Oracle database management is the first major part of an Oracle DBA's job. It involves three key tasks: maintaining existing databases, putting up new databases, and fixing broken ones. This section takes a systematic approach to database maintenance and management. It contains checklists that will help you develop a database management regimen, avoid costly errors when it comes time to move a database into production, and assist with database recovery when trouble strikes and you lose a database object.

Performing Routine DBA Procedures

Some DBA tasks need to be performed on a regular basis, others in response to emergencies or specific user needs.

The checklists in the following sections will help you perform routine checks on the status of each of your Oracle databases on a daily, weekly, and monthly basis.

NOTE

Some of these DBA procedures have been automated with SQL*Plus scripts. You can download a copy of the procedures and scripts from the RevealNet web site at *http://www.revealnet.com/Pipelines/DBA/archives.htm#code28.*

Daily DBA procedures

This section summarizes the procedures we recommend you follow on a daily basis to check the status of each of your Oracle databases:

1. Verify that all instances are up.

   Make sure the databases are available. Log in to each instance and run daily reports or test scripts. Some sites may want you to automate this step. As an option, consider using Oracle Enterprise Manager's *probe* event.

2. Look for any new alert log entries by doing the following:

   - Connect to each managed system. Use Telnet, SSH, or a similar protocol to connect.
   - For each managed instance, go to the background dump destination (usually *$ORACLE_BASE/<SID>/bdump*, where *<SID>* is the database system identifier, or SID). Make sure to look under the SID for each database you are managing.
   - At the prompt, use the Unix *tail* command to check the *alert_<SID>.log*, or examine the most recent entries in the alert log file in some other way.
   - If any ORA errors have appeared since the last time you looked, note them in your Database Recovery

Log and investigate each one. The Database Recovery Log is a text file you should create and maintain; there you can record for future reference any problems you find and any actions you take.

3. Verify that the Simple Network Management Protocol (SNMP) subagent for the Oracle database, *dbsnmp*, is running:

   – Log on to each machine you are managing, to check for the *dbsnmp* process.

   – For Unix, at the command line, type:

     ```
     ps -ef | grep dbsnmp
     ```

   There should be two *dbsnmp* processes running. If not, restart *dbsnmp*.

4. Verify that the database backup was successful.

5. Verify that the database archiving to tape was successful.

6. Verify that you have enough resources for acceptable performance by doing the following:

   – Verify free space in tablespaces.

   For each instance, make sure that enough free space exists in each tablespace to handle the day's expected growth. When incoming data is stable and the average daily growth can be calculated, your minimum free space should at least equal the amount of data growth you expect during the time it will take to order, receive, and install additional disks.

   – Verify rollback segments as follows:

     i. To obtain the current status of each ONLINE or FULL rollback segment (by ID, not by name), query on the V$ROLLSTAT view.

     ii. Status should be ONLINE, not OFFLINE or FULL, except in those cases in which you have a special rollback segment for large batch jobs whose normal status is OFFLINE.

iii. Optional: for each database you may have a list of rollback segment names and their expected statuses.

iv. For storage parameters and names of all rollback segments, query on DBA_ROLLBACK_SEGS. This view's STATUS field is less accurate than V$ROLLSTAT, however, since it lacks the PENDING OFFLINE and FULL statuses; it shows these as OFFLINE and ONLINE, respectively.

– Identify bad growth projections:

i. Gather daily sizing information.

ii. Check current extents.

iii. Query current table sizing information.

iv. Query current index sizing information.

v. Query growth trends.

Look for segments in the database that are running out of resources (e.g., extents) or growing at an excessive rate. You may need to adjust the storage parameters of these segments. For example, if any object has reached 200 as the number of current extents, upgrade the MAX_EXTENTS parameter in the *INIT.ORA* file to a value of UNLIMITED.

– Identify space-bound objects.

The NEXT_EXTENT values for space-bound objects are bigger than the largest extent that the tablespace can offer. Space-bound objects can harm database performance. If you encounter such objects, you first need to investigate the situation. Then you can either add another datafile or manually defragment the tablespace using the COALESCE clause of the ALTER TABLESPACE command:

```
ALTER TABLESPACE name COALESCE
```

where *name* is the tablespace name.

- Be sure to review contention for CPU, memory, network, and disk resources.

7. As a final daily requirement, keep improving your overall DBA skills by spending at least one hour a day reading your DBA manuals.

Weekly DBA procedures

This section summarizes the procedures we recommend you follow on a weekly basis to check the status of each of your Oracle databases:

1. Look for objects that break rules.

   For each object-creation policy (naming convention, storage parameter, etc.), institute an automated check to verify that the policy is being followed. Make sure every object in a given tablespace has the exact same size for NEXT_EXTENT and that this value matches the tablespace default for its NEXT_EXTENT parameter value.

2. Ensure that all tables have unique primary keys:
   - Check for missing primary keys.
   - Check for disabled primary keys.
   - Make sure all primary key indexes are unique.
3. Ensure that all indexes use an index tablespace.
4. Ensure that schemas look identical between environments (especially test and production environments):
   - Check for datatype consistency.
   - Check for the consistency of other objects.
5. Look for security policy violations.
6. Look in Net8 logs for errors and other issues.
7. Archive all alert logs to history.

Monthly DBA procedures

This section summarizes the procedures we recommend you follow on a monthly basis to check the status of each of your Oracle databases:

1. Look for harmful growth rates.

   Review changes in segment growth, as compared to previous reports, to identify segments that may be growing in a harmful way.

2. Examine tuning opportunities.

   Review common Oracle tuning points, such as cache hit ratio, latch contention, and other points dealing with memory management. Compare these with past reports to identify harmful trends and determine the impact of recent tuning adjustments.

3. Look for I/O contention.

   Review database file activity. Compare this activity to past output to identify trends that could lead to possible contention.

4. Review fragmentation by investigating row chaining and other areas of fragmentation.

5. Project performance into the future as follows:

   - Compare reports on CPU, memory, network, and disk utilization from both Oracle and the operating system to identify trends that could lead to contention for any one of these resources in the near future.

   - Compare performance trends to your organization's Service Level Agreement to see when your system will go out of bounds.

6. Perform tuning and maintenance.

   Make whatever adjustments are necessary to avoid contention for system resources. These adjustments may include scheduled downtime or requests for additional resources.

Preparing a Database for Production

Far too often, DBAs put databases into production without really making sure they're ready. The purpose of the checklists in the following sections is to provide a quick list of things you should double-check to ensure that your database has a solid foundation for performance and availability.

Essentially, there are two parts to any database: the core database and the application schema. Check both of them carefully before putting the database into production.

Core database

The core Oracle database is the basic database, not including any application-specific objects. It contains:

1. Everything created when the CREATE DATABASE command is issued, including:
   - The SYSTEM tablespace
   - The redo log files
   - The control files
   - The internal tables (via Oracle's *sql.bsq* script)
   - The SYS and SYSTEM user IDs (via Oracle's *sql.bsq* script)
2. The Oracle data dictionary, created with Oracle's scripts (*catalog.sql*, *catproc.sql*, *catblock.sql*, etc.)
3. The configuration files (*INIT.ORA* and *CONFIG.ORA*)
4. The rollback segment tablespaces (containing all public rollback segments)
5. The temporary segment tablespaces (typically called TEMP, TEMP_TS, TEMPORARY_DATA, etc.); these are

used by Oracle to store intermediate results of queries—for example, when sorting data

6. The default user tablespaces (typically called USERS, USERS_TS, USER_DATA, etc.)

Core database checklist

Follow this checklist to make sure the core database is ready to be put into production:

1. Perform the necessary preparation:
   - Has the database been designed properly?
   - Does the server have enough capacity for this database?
   - Are there backup/recovery capabilities on the server?
2. Create the core database:
   - Has the DB_BLOCK_SIZE parameter been set correctly? Note that this parameter cannot be modified simply by changing the *INIT.ORA* parameter and cycling the database. The DB_BLOCK_SIZE parameter, like many of the core database parameters, should never be altered after database creation unless the database is recreated.
   - Has the DB_NAME parameter been set correctly? This parameter also cannot be modified simply by changing the *INIT.ORA* parameter and cycling the database.
   - Has the NLS_CHARACTER_SET parameter been set correctly? This parameter also cannot be modified simply by changing the *INIT.ORA* parameter and cycling the database.
   - Has the location of the alert log been determined and set? Problems may occur when the database is created or even when it's up and running, and the

alert log file is needed to capture system-type error messages.

- Are there multiple copies of the control file, mirrored on separate disk drives?
- Is the SYSTEM tablespace adequately sized?
- Are there at least three redo log groups (one in use, one waiting to be used, and one archiving)?
- Are the redo log files adequately sized? You should start each group at a minimum of 1–5 MB and monitor redo log switches. If a log switch to a redo log that is being archived occurs, the database stops.
- Are the redo log groups mirrored?
- Are the various MAX parameters (e.g., MAXLOGFILES) set correctly for the type of database being built?
- Does the database need to be running in archivelog mode?

3. Complete the core database:
   - Have the data dictionary scripts been run? At minimum, these include *catalog.sql*, *catproc.sql*, and *catblock.sql*.
   - Is there a separate tablespace (or tablespaces) for *only* temporary segments?
   - Is the temporary tablespace defined as type TEMPORARY?
   - Is the temporary tablespace adequately sized? At minimum, this tablespace should be as large as the largest index that will be created, plus 10% for overhead.
   - Is there a separate tablespace (or tablespaces) for *only* rollback segments?

- Are the rollback segment tablespaces adequately sized?
- Are the storage parameters for the rollback segments set correctly?
- Is SYS (and maybe SYSTEM) the only owner of objects created in the SYSTEM tablespace?
- Was the *pupbld.sql* script run under the SYSTEM schema?

4. Provide all user definitions:
   - Do all users have their DEFAULT and TEMPORARY tablespaces set correctly?
   - Do users have quotas defined on their DEFAULT tablespaces?
   - Are profiles necessary for this database?
5. Establish basic security:
   - Have the default account passwords (especially SYS, SYSTEM, and INTERNAL) been changed from their install defaults?
   - Is the DBA role protected from use by anyone except the instance administrator?
   - Are all end-user system privileges granted through database roles?
6. Check the following after database implementation:
   - Has the database been added to the backup routine?
   - Has a procedure been implemented for periodically checking for corrupt data blocks?
   - Has the System Global Area (SGA) been adequately sized?

Application schema

Many application schemas can reside in one core database. Each application schema contains several types of application-specific objects, such as:

- Views
- Sequences
- Database triggers
- Referential integrity objects
- Functions
- Tables
- Indexes
- Packages
- Procedures

In addition to the schema-specific object types listed here, you'll often have public database synonyms that point to various schema objects. These will be necessary for your applications even though they aren't, strictly speaking, part of their schemas.

The tablespace is another form of application-specific object created at the database level. You'll generally need table and index tablespaces for each schema you create.

Application schema checklist

Follow this checklist to make sure your application schemas are ready to be put into production:

1. Perform physical configuration:
   - Does each application have its own schema?
   - Does each schema have its own set of table and index tablespaces?
   - Are tables and their corresponding indexes in separate tablespaces?

2. Check on performance issues:
   - If you are implementing referential integrity, are all core foreign keys indexed?
   - Are there tables without indexes?
   - Are there tables with too many indexes?
   - Are there tables with similar indexes?
   - Are the schema objects regularly analyzed?
3. Check on security issues:
   - Are all object grants performed through roles? (While doing this is not strictly necessary, it does make administration much easier.)
   - If your applications allow for it, are all updating capabilities granted through nondefault roles?
4. Check on miscellaneous issues:
   - Are naming conventions in place for all database objects? (While using consistent naming conventions is not strictly necessary, it does make administration much easier.)
   - Is the value of the PCTINCREASE parameter for each tablespace greater than 0? This will ensure the automatic coalescing of free space. If you do not want your extent sizes to change, you'll want to ensure that PCTINCREASE is set to 0.

Performing Backup and Recovery

Sooner or later, every DBA will face the challenge of having to restore a lost object. The object may be lost from a test system where time is not of the essence or, much worse, from a production system where every second counts. Recovery generally is required only after some physical insult to the database filesystem has occurred. Most internal errors are corrected automatically using Oracle's redo logs.

The particular recovery steps for your system will depend entirely upon how you performed your most recent backup and what needs to be recovered. However, you can use this section as a quick reference to the various database recovery options. Select the options you need based on the particular type of failure that has occurred.

Disk setup

To recover your Oracle database from various system failures you have to know how the system is physically configured on the disks. In the following discussion of recovery procedures, we assume that you have spread the Oracle files across several platters to reduce disk contention and to speed up access. Our example configuration is shown in Table 1.

Table 1. Sample Disk Layout

Physical Disks	Directory	Contents
1	*/oracle0*	Executables, forms, reports, menus, shell scripts, one control file, trace files, logs, redo logs
2	*/oracle1*	Datafiles (including those for the SYSTEM tablespace), one copy of the control file, the temporary tablespace(s)
3	*/oracle2*	Another copy of the control file, indexes
4	*/oracle3*	Rollback segments, exports
5	*/oracle4*	All archive logs

The following list summarizes the recovery needed after failure of each of your disks:

Loss of /oracle0

Losing */oracle0* means the system administrator will have to perform a restore operation (from backup tapes) to recover the system's executables, shell scripts (command files), forms, reports, menus, log files, redo log files, trace files, and the most recent control file. If any changes to the database structure have occurred since the last backup, the control file will contain out-of-date information and will have to be copied from an unaffected disk before you start the instance. This is necessary because the control file contains the latest description of archive log usage and datafile locations. The loss of redo log files will require a recovery to the most current archive log file. If the affected redo logs were online at the time of the loss and no mirroring was used, some data loss will occur.

Loss of /oracle1

Losing */oracle1* is the most serious type of loss, because */oracle1* contains the majority of the datafiles. To recover, you will have to restore from the most current backup. You will then need to apply all archive logs from the last backup to the current date. An alternative method of recovery is to recreate the database, import the most recent full export, and then apply all cumulative and incremental exports. However, a restore from imports is current only to the date and time of the last export file applied, and no further recovery is possible. Recovery of the redo log files will be automatic. If the affected redo logs were online at the time of the loss and no mirroring was used, data loss will occur.

Loss of /oracle2

Losing */oracle2* will slow data access but will not necessarily require immediate recovery. If the index tablespaces are taken offline (using commands issued from SQL*Plus), users will still be able to access the data for query-only operations in the database, since indexes are not required for these operations. However, updates involving indexed tables will not be possible. You can recover the index tablespaces using the archive logs and the tablespace recovery procedure. If the affected redo logs were online at the time of the loss and no mirroring was used, some data loss will occur.

Loss of /oracle3

Losing */oracle3* will result in the loss of uncommitted DML statements. Using redo and archive logs, you will be able to bring the database back to the way it was when the crash occurred, but crash recovery will roll back any uncommitted statements. The loss of export files in */oracle3* also means you will have to export the database as soon as possible, so you will have a fresh, reliable export file.

Loss of /oracle4

Losing */oracle4* will require an immediate Oracle shutdown and a full backup or full export followed by a shutdown. Doing this is the only way to ensure data recoverability if you haven't been able to recover lost archives and exports. You can then reset the archive log destination and restart Oracle. If immediate shutdown is not possible, you can reset the archive log destination and continue operation. This method is not a safe condition for full recovery, but it will allow continued use until you can perform a full backup.

Note that since the backup of your archive disk is one week old, it is useless. Only those archive logs created since the last backup are needed for recovery. When you shut down and back up the database, the lost archive logs become irrelevant.

Loss of a single file

If a user loses data because he has deleted a table inadvertently, you can recover the table from the last full export or the last incremental export that contains the table, up to the day prior to the loss. If exports have not been taken, however, recovery of a single table will require restoring the entire tablespace and applying archive logs up to the time just prior to the table loss (this requires the tablespace to be offline).

Partial disk loss

If you lose only a small section of a disk, recovery will depend on the type of Oracle file that occupied that area of the disk.

Nonphysical data problems

Other than physical data loss (e.g., a disk crash), all other recovery scenarios are handled automatically by the Oracle kernel. These include program failure, instance failure due to a bug, and system failure due to power loss or a forced crash.

The following sections contain checklists you can use in recovering different types of files.

Recover from loss of a single tablespace's datafile

1. Log in as the *oracle* operating system user.
2. If the tablespace that uses the datafile is online, take it offline by issuing the following commands from SQL*Plus:

   ```
   CONNECT INTERNAL
   ALTER TABLESPACE name OFFLINE
   ```

   where *name* is the tablespace name—for example, DEV or PROD.
3. Correct the problem, or find a new location for the file(s).
4. Have the system administrator recover the latest copy of the lost datafile from the latest Oracle backup tape into the selected location.
5. If the file had to be relocated, alter the name in the database, using the following command to make the change:

   ```
   ALTER DATABASE RENAME FILE 'old' TO 'new'
   ```

   where *old* and *new* are full path filenames enclosed in single quotes.

6. Execute the RECOVER command from SQL*Plus using the TABLESPACE option as follows:

   ```
   RECOVER TABLESPACE name
   ```

   where *name* is the tablespace name.

   Oracle will prompt for the names of the necessary archive files, beginning with the oldest file. All required logs should be accessible by Oracle.

7. Once all logs have been applied to the affected tablespace, the system will respond as follows:

   ```
   Media recovery complete.
   ```

8. Bring the tablespace back online by issuing the following command from SQL*Plus:

   ```
   ALTER TABLESPACE name ONLINE
   ```

Recover a deleted table

1. If possible, determine from the user when the table was deleted and when the last modifications were made.

2. Log in as the *oracle* operating system user, and get a list of the full export files and the incremental export files on the system. If a full export has been done since the last update, but before the file was deleted, use this file in step 4.

3. From the list of incremental exports, determine the export that was made just after the date the table was last modified but before the date the table was deleted. If the date of modification and deletion are the same, select the latest export file prior to the table's deletion. If there is no export file on the system, have the system administrator restore the contents of the export directory (*/oracle3/ORTEST1/admin/exports* in our examples) from the last system backup, and then check the export file again. If the export file still is not available, repeat the restore request with the system backup previous to

the one used in the last attempt. If the export file needed is not on the available backups, the table cannot be imported. If the table has not been modified, it will not be in any incremental export and must be imported from a full export file.

4. Once a suitable export is located, set the default directory to the export file location using the command:

```
cd /oracle3/ORTEST1/admin/exports
```

5. Use the following import command from the system prompt to restore the table:

```
imp SYSTEM/password FROMUSER=user TOUSER=user
  TABLES=(table_name) FILE=export_file_name
```

where:

– *password* is the SYSTEM password of the DBA user

– *user* is the table owner's username

– *table_name* is the name of the table to be imported

– *export_file_name* is the name of the export file

This imports the table as it was on the creation date of the export file. If data was added or removed from the table since this export occurred, you will have to enter that data again. This may result in loss of referential integrity, so you may need to disable any referential integrity constraints until the data is fully restored.

Recover from loss of executables and control file

In our example, since */oracle0* contains all the executable files and system tablespace datafiles, database activity will cease if */oracle0* is lost. In this event, do the following:

1. Shut down the database with the IMMEDIATE option.
2. Have the system administrator restore the */oracle0/ORTEST1/** directory structures from the latest backup.

3. Copy one of the remaining control files over the lost control file (*/oracle1/ORTEST1/control/ora_control3.con* or */oracle2/ORTEST1/control/ora_control2.con*).
4. Restart the instance using the STARTUP MOUNT command.
5. Use your procedure for total database recovery to restore the SYSTEM tablespace, which requires a full database restore to recover.

Recover from loss of datafiles and/or index files

Use the following procedure to recover from the loss of a datafile or index file from a tablespace. It doesn't matter whether the tablespace is used to store data from a table or from an index. Here are the steps:

1. Log in as the *oracle* operating system user.
2. Start up SQL*Plus and CONNECT INTERNAL.
3. Issue the SHUTDOWN ABORT command.
4. Have the system administrator restore the lost datafiles and/or index files.
5. Issue the following command from SQL*Plus to restart the instance:

   ```
   STARTUP MOUNT database_name
   ```

6. If the failure caused the affected files to be relocated, you must rename the files using the following command from SQL*Plus:

   ```
   ALTER DATABASE RENAME FILE 'old' TO 'new'
   ```

   where `old` and `new` are the full path filenames, enclosed in single quotes, for each of the affected files.

7. Issue the RECOVER DATABASE command and apply all needed archive log files.

   Oracle will prompt for the names of the necessary archive files, beginning with the oldest file. All required logs should be online. After each log is applied, the system will prompt for the next one it requires. After the last one has been applied, the system will respond:

```
Media recovery complete.
```

This concludes the recovery.

8. To ensure that all database files are online, issue the following command for each of the affected database files:

   ```
   ALTER DATABASE DATAFILE 'name' ONLINE
   ```

   where *name* is the full path filename enclosed in single quotes.

9. The database can now be opened by issuing the following ALTER DATABASE command:

   ```
   ALTER DATABASE [name] OPEN
   ```

   In some cases, you will not need to specify the database name in this command. If you omit the name, Oracle assumes that you want to alter the database identified by the value of the DB_NAME initialization parameter.

Recover from loss of all rollback segments

1. Log in as the *oracle* operating system user.
2. Use the editor of your choice to alter the instance initialization file (our example uses the */oracle0/ORTEST1/admin/pfile* directory) to comment out the ROLLBACK_SEGMENTS entry. This prevents the system from trying to acquire on restart anything but the rollback segment contained in the SYSTEM tablespace.
3. Shut down and restart the instance by issuing commands from SQL*Plus.
4. Create a second rollback segment by issuing the following command from SQL*Plus:

   ```
   CREATE ROLLBACK SEGMENT segment_name
      TABLESPACE tablespace_name
   ```

where *segment_name* is the name of the rollback segment (for example, ROLLBACK_1) and *tablespace_name* is any tablespace for the rollback segment. You can use almost any tablespace for this purpose, even SYSTEM, because this segment is only temporary. However, do not use the old rollback segment tablespace, because you are going to drop it. Since this segment will be dropped later, use the default storage parameters.

5. Alter the instance initialization file */oracle0/ORTEST1/admin/pfile* by adding a new ROLLBACK_SEGMENTS entry to list only the name of the segment created in step 4.

6. Shut down and restart the instance by issuing commands from SQL*Plus.

7. Drop the old rollback segment tablespace as follows:

   ```
   DROP TABLESPACE ROLLBACK_SEGS INCLUDING CONTENTS
   ```

8. Use a CREATE TABLESPACE command such as the following to create a new rollback segment tablespace:

   ```
   CREATE TABLESPACE ROLLBACK_SEGS
      DATAFILE 'file spec' SIZE 100M [REUSE]
      DEFAULT STORAGE (
         INITIAL 500K NEXT 500K
         MAXEXTENTS 99)
      ONLINE
   ```

   If the location is the same, use the REUSE option on the *file spec*. The size will be the same as before.

9. Using the original rollback-creation script (if available), rebuild the rollback segments. If the original script is not available, you will need to manually recreate the rollback segments as they initially existed.

10. Shut down the database; then edit the initialization file to return it to the condition it was in before the loss of the rollback segments.

11. Restart the database.

12. Drop the rollback segment you created in the SYSTEM tablespace. This completes the recovery from the loss of the rollback segments.

13. If you're using the same disk for rollback segments and export files (as we are in our example database), you'll need to perform a full export because your earlier export files will have been lost.

Recover from loss of an active rollback segment

1. Log in as the *oracle* operating system user.

2. Open the initialization file in an editor, and add the following line:

   ```
   _OFFLINE_ROLLBACK_SEGMENTS=(name)
   ```

   where *name* is the name of the lost rollback segment.

3. While still in the editor, remove the reference to the lost rollback segment from the ROLLBACK_SEGMENTS entry in the initialization file. Save the file and exit the editor.

4. Shut down and restart the database by issuing commands from SQL*Plus. Note that you can attempt to take the rollback segment offline with the command:

   ```
   ALTER ROLLBACK SEGMENT name OFFLINE
   ```

   However, this may not always work.

5. Drop the corrupted rollback segment using the following SQL*Plus commands:

   ```
   CONNECT INTERNAL
   DROP ROLLBACK SEGMENT name
   ```

6. Recreate the rollback segment using a command such as the following:

   ```
   CREATE ROLLBACK SEGMENT name
      TABLESPACE ROLLBACK_SEGS
      STORAGE (INITIAL 500K
               NEXT 500K
               MAXEXTENTS 99)
   ```

7. Edit the initialization file to remove the _OFFLINE_ROLLBACK_SEGMENTS line and add back the name of the rollback segment in the ROLLBACK_SEGMENTS entry. Exit the editor.

8. Shut down and restart the database by issuing commands from SQL*Plus. Alternatively, you can bring the rollback segment online using the command:

   ```
   ALTER ROLLBACK SEGMENT name ONLINE
   ```

   We recommend, however, that you go through a shutdown/restart cycle so you can verify that the initialization file changes have been made properly.

9. After you've completed this procedure, check the integrity of the database using the following steps:

   a. Set the default to the export directory:

      ```
      cd /oracle3/ORTEST1/admin/exports
      ```

   b. Issue the following export command:

      ```
      exp SYSTEM/[password] FULL=YES INDEXES=YES
         ROWS=NO
      ```

   If no errors are returned, the database is consistent. If errors are returned, use the RECOVER DATABASE command to recover the database. Usually the startup/shutdown cycle will catch and correct any problems.

Recover from loss of an inactive redo log file

1. Log in as the *oracle* operating system user.

2. Start SQL*Plus and issue the following commands:

   ```
   CONNECT INTERNAL
   SHUTDOWN ABORT
   ```

3. Exit out to the operating system and copy another member of that group or a backup copy of the damaged file to the location of the lost file. If none are available, ask your system administrator to retrieve this file from a system archive.

4. Use SQL*Plus to issue the following commands:

```
CONNECT INTERNAL
STARTUP MOUNT
```

5. If the failure was a result of media damage (which requires moving the redo log file to a different disk), rename the log file using the following ALTER DATABASE command:

```
ALTER DATABASE RENAME FILE 'old' TO 'new'
```

where *old* and *new* are the full path filenames enclosed in single quotes.

6. Issue the following command from SQL*Plus:

```
ALTER DATABASE OPEN
```

7. If step 6 was successful, continue on to step 8. If step 6 was unsuccessful, verify that you used the correct archival copy in step 3. Repeat steps 1 through 6 if you used the wrong file. Otherwise, continue on to step 9.

8. Using SQL*Plus, shut down the Oracle database, and have the system administrator perform a full backup of the Oracle system. Recovery is now complete. Do *not* proceed beyond this step.

NOTE

Perform steps 9 and higher only if step 6 was unsuccessful.

---

9. Using SQL*Plus, start the database in mount mode and stop archiving with these commands:

```
CONNECT INTERNAL
STARTUP MOUNT
ALTER DATABASE NOARCHIVELOG
```

10. Using SQL*Plus, replace the lost redo log file with a new one using the following command:

```
ALTER DATABASE ADD LOGFILE MEMBER
    'new_file' to group 'integer number'
```

where *new_file* is the full path filename, enclosed in single quotes.

11. Still using SQL*Plus, drop the damaged file using the command:

    ```
    ALTER DATABASE DROP LOGFILE MEMBER 'old_name'
    ```

    where *old_name* is the full path filename, enclosed in single quotes. If this results in an error, go to the procedure for recovering from the loss of an active redo log file.

12. Exit from SQL*Plus and have the system administrator back up all the redo logs, including the one created in step 10.

13. Back up the current control file using commands issued from SQL*Plus:

    ```
    CONNECT INTERNAL
    ALTER DATABASE BACKUP CONTROL FILE TO 'backup_file'
    ```

    where *backup_file* is a full path filename, enclosed in single quotes.

14. Using commands issued from SQL*Plus, shut down the database and have the system administrator back up the database files.

15. Restart the database. Issue the following commands from SQL*Plus:

    ```
    CONNECT INTERNAL
    STARTUP
    ALTER DATABASE ARCHIVELOG
    ```

16. Issue the following commands to shut down and restart the database:

    ```
    SHUTDOWN
    STARTUP OPEN
    ```

    If this results in an error, go to the procedure for recovering an active redo log.

In some situations, the current redo log may become corrupt and, if it is the only log required for recovery, you will not be able to recover even with CANCEL-based recovery.

Recover from loss of an active redo log file

1. Log in as the *oracle* operating system user.
2. Shut down the database using the following SQL*Plus commands:

   ```
   CONNECT INTERNAL
   SHUTDOWN ABORT
   ```

3. Exit from SQL*Plus and have the system administrator back up all database files. This provides you with a restart point in case the rest of the recovery fails.
4. Correct the problem that caused the failure, or find a new location for the redo logs.
5. Have the system administrator restore all database files using the latest backup, but not the backup from step 3.
6. Start the database and mount it by issuing the following commands from SQL*Plus:

   ```
   CONNECT INTERNAL
   STARTUP MOUNT
   ```

7. Make sure all database files are online by executing the following command for each file:

   ```
   ALTER DATABASE DATAFILE 'name' ONLINE
   ```

   where *name* is the full path filename, enclosed in single quotes. If a database is recovered with a datafile offline, that file's data is lost.
8. If the original location of the redo logs has become invalid, rename the files with the following command issued from SQL*Plus:

   ```
   ALTER DATABASE RENAME FILE 'old' TO 'new'
   ```

where *old* and *new* are full path filenames enclosed in single quotes. Each file must be renamed if its location has changed.

9. Recover the database in manual mode using the command:

```
RECOVER DATABASE MANUAL
```

   Oracle will prompt for the names of the required archive files, beginning with the oldest file. All required logs should be online. After each log is applied, the system will request the next one in the sequence. When the log just prior to the damaged log is applied, issue the CANCEL command to abort the recovery operation. At this point, recovery is complete. All data in the damaged redo log is lost and must be reentered.

10. Restart the database by issuing the following command from SQL*Plus:

```
ALTER DATABASE OPEN RESETLOGS
```

   The RESETLOGS option will initialize the set of redo logs and start a new sequence of archive log files.

11. Once the database is open, immediately shut it down by issuing one of these commands from SQL*Plus:

```
SHUTDOWN
SHUTDOWN IMMEDIATE
```

12. Exit from SQL*Plus and have the system administrator make a complete backup of the Oracle system. All previous archive logs are now invalid and may be disposed of.

13. Using SQL*Plus, restart the Oracle instance.

Recover from loss of archive logs

If you have lost the archive logs and the system administrator is able to fix the problem, shut down the system. Have the system administrator perform a full backup and then restart Oracle. If the system administrator cannot fix the problem and a new archive log location is set up, perform the following steps:

1. Using SQL*Plus, issue the following commands:

   ```
   CONNECT INTERNAL
   ARCHIVE LOG 'dest'
   ```

   where *dest* is the new location. For example, if the new location is */oracle5/ORTEST1/admin/arch*, `dest` would be `/oracle5/ORTEST1/admin/arch`.

2. Exit from SQL*Plus, and edit the initialization file to reflect the new archive log location by changing the LOG_ARCHIVE_DEST parameter.

3. Using SQL*Plus, shut down the Oracle system.

4. Have the system administrator perform a full backup of the Oracle system; then use commands issued from SQL*Plus to restart the database instance using the RESETLOG option.

Recover from loss of all control files

If, for some unimaginable reason, you lose all copies of your control file, there is a CREATE CONTROLFILE command available to rebuild them. In reality, if you follow Oracle Flexible Architecture (OFA) guidelines, practically the only way this could happen is through deliberate sabotage.

You must know the following information in order to rebuild the control file:

1. All redo log filenames and locations
2. All database file datafiles and locations
3. The values for the MAXLOGFILES, MAXDATAFILES, and MAXINSTANCES parameters
4. The status of archive logging

Items 1, 2, and 3 should be available via the original *CREATE_<db_name>* script. Make sure you document these items before you need them.

Any datafile containing a rollback segment must be available, or recovery will fail. Use the following procedure to rebuild the control file:

1. Back up all existing files.
2. Start up SQL*Plus.
3. Issue the STARTUP NOMOUNT command.
4. Issue the CREATE CONTROLFILE command.
5. Issue the ALTER DATABASE MOUNT command.
6. Apply the required recovery to the database files. Use the RECOVER DATABASE command.
7. Shut down cleanly (issue SHUTDOWN with no options or SHUTDOWN IMMEDIATE).
8. Back up the recovered database.
9. Restart the database.

To be proactive, every time you make a change to the physical structure of a database that affects your control file, you should issue the following command:

```
ALTER DATABASE BACKUP CONTROLFILE TO TRACE
```

This command will generate a script that will, with minimal editing later on, allow you to recreate your control file. The script must be generated before there is a problem. The output from the command will be placed in a trace file located in the directory specified in the BACKGROUND_DUMP_DEST parameter in the initialization file for the instance.

Installation and Configuration

Oracle installation and configuration comprise the second major part of an Oracle DBA's job. The installation and configuration process can be complex and is very platform-specific. Nevertheless, there are many universal topics involving structure and layout, and we've collected information about these topics in this section. Where appropriate, we've included material for specific platforms as well.

The topics in this section are not intended to replace the *Installation and User's Guide* for your Oracle system. The material here is designed to supply general guidance and recommendations for the items you must consider when you are configuring and/or migrating your Oracle software.

Installing Oracle on Unix

The Unix operating system varies considerably from platform to platform. This makes it difficult, if not impossible, to write a generic installation procedure for Unix. We strongly suggest that you use the installation guide provided by Oracle for your own site's release of Unix. The following procedure is a general set of guidelines and is *not* intended to replace Oracle's installation procedures:

1. Review all installation documents distributed with your software.

2. Ensure that all requirements specified in the documentation have been met.

   Using the guides provided in the documentation, establish the proper operating system environment. Be sure to coordinate with your system administrator regarding all changes to the shared memory.

3. Create the Oracle DBA account.

   Prepare a detailed description of all Oracle DBA account requirements, and give it to the system administrator. (This description must include explanations of the reasons behind the requirements.) Have the system administrator create the required account.

NOTE

The Oracle DBA account, which is usually named *oracle*, must belong to the DBA group. The DBA group is usually named *dba*.

4. Ensure that disk space and access requirements are met.

   Have the system administrator review the available disks for space availability, speed of access, and fragmentation status. If necessary, have the system administrator defragment the disks. (Defragmentation is required because Oracle requires contiguous files.)

5. Create an installation map.

   Obtain information about the disks, their speeds, and their available capacities from the system administrator. Using the charts provided for your system in your Oracle installation guide, determine your disk and memory requirements and prepare an installation map showing file placement.

6. Determine how many users will be using the database, and write down this number.

7. Determine how many redo logs, groups, and members in a group you will need, and write down these numbers.

8. Determine how many rollback segments you will need, and write down this number.

9. Determine the disks on which you want to place the control files, and write down these locations.

10. Determine what you want to call your instance (SID), and write down this name. The name can be up to six characters long.

11. Determine what you want to call your database, and write down this name. The name can be up to eight characters long.

12. Write down the number, size, and location of the datafiles you will need.

    You will need at least five datafiles, plus two more for each application. Write down what size they should be in megabytes. Map out their locations if you have more than one data disk. Determine whether you have any large tables that might require their own tablespace areas. If you are using raw devices, map out their placement.

13. Determine where you want your archive logs written, and write down this location.

14. Determine where you want to store exports, and write down this location.

15. Make a list of your initial users, along with their default applications, and note any users that require the ability to create tables.

16. Use the installation checklists for your system once you have the required information gathered in one place.

NOTE

Because of the differences for each release of Unix that Oracle supports, we can't cover every possible variation on the installation procedure here.

---

17. Insert the Oracle8*i* CD-ROM and run the installation procedure described in Oracle's *Installation and User's Guide* (including all preinstallation and postinstallation activity).

18. Once the base install is complete, add control files, tablespaces, redo logs, and rollback segments as follows:

    a. Log on as the *oracle* user. Then issue the CONNECT INTERNAL command to become the SYS user.

b. Use the CREATE ROLLBACK SEGMENT command to add a second rollback segment to the SYSTEM tablespace.

c. As the SYS user, issue the ALTER ROLLBACK SEGMENT command to bring the rollback segment just created online.

19. Add the additional tablespaces you need. You can do this with the CREATE TABLESPACE command.

NOTE

For documentation purposes, to save you from having to enter the commands over and over again, and to reduce the chance of error, we suggest that you create a SQL script to create these initial tablespaces.

---

20. Add the required number of rollback segments, and place them in their own tablespace.

21. Shut down the database, open the *INIT.ORA* file in an editor, and place the names of the new rollback segments in the ROLLBACK_SEGMENTS parameter entry.

22. Restart the instance.

23. Set up the tools tablespace.

24. Change the default passwords. The default passwords assigned during startup are:

    – For the INTERNAL user (the ID used to start up the databases): "oracle"

    – For the SYS user: "change_on_install"

    – For the SYSTEM user: "manager"

    Change these passwords as soon as possible; if you don't, you will be leaving a significant security hole in your database.

Installing Oracle on Windows NT

Follow these steps to install Oracle on a Windows NT system. You must configure the server as an application server—not a file server—or performance will not be acceptable. You can do this at the time of initial server setup, or you can alter the configuration later on. We've supplied only a general set of guidelines here, and the instructions are not intended to replace the installation procedures provided by Oracle:

1. Review all installation documents distributed with your software.

2. Ensure that all requirements specified in the documentation have been met.

   Using the guides provided in the documentation, establish the proper operating system environment. Ensure that enough disk space is available on all the drives on which you will need to install Oracle and build your database.

3. Create the Oracle DBA account.

   Provide a detailed description of all Oracle DBA account requirements and give it to the system administrator. In most cases in a Windows NT environment, this will be you. Essentially, the requirements are that the user be in the *administrators* group and have share/write capabilities on all disks required for the installation.

4. Ensure that disk space and access requirements are met.

   Have the system administrator review the available disks for space availability, speed of access, and fragmentation status. If necessary, have the system administrator defragment the disks. (Defragmentation is required because Oracle requires contiguous files.)

5. Create an installation map.

   To do this, you'll need to obtain information from the system administrator about the disks, their speeds, and their available capacities. Using this information, prepare an installation map showing file placement. In terms of the disk space requirements for Oracle8*i* code, the 8.1 code footprint on a Windows NT 4.0 platform is 164 MB, including a 36-MB example database.

6. Define the required directory structure on each disk. The structure should start with a generic top-level directory, such as *oracle8*, and have subdirectories for each application. If you wish, you can use the Oracle convention of DB_ followed by the SID name of the database to name these directories.

   Within these subdirectories, it might be advisable to further subdivide each directory into file types (if multiple file types will be stored there). Remember that if you have fewer than five disks available, you can still assign five or more subdirectories in preparation for the time when you may have more room to spread the files.

7. Determine how many users will be using the database, and write down this number.

8. Determine how many redo log groups and group members you will need, and write down these numbers.

9. Determine how many rollback segments you will need, and write down this number.

10. Determine the disks on which you want to place control files, and write down these locations.

11. Determine what you want to call your instance (SID), and write down this name. For versions up to Oracle 8.0, the name can be up to four characters long. Since Oracle8*i*, the SID can be up to 64 alphanumeric characters long.

12. Determine what you want to call your database, and write down this name. The name can be up to 64 characters long.
13. Determine how many tablespaces you will need, and write down this number. You will need at least five tablespaces, plus two more for each application. Write down what size they should be in megabytes. Map out their locations if you have more than one data disk, and determine whether you have any large tables that might require their own tablespace areas. It has been reported that Oracle prefers 500-MB datafiles, so it's best to use datafiles of that size to make up your new tablespaces. This is also an easier size to back up to tape and move from disk to disk if necessary.
14. Determine where you want your archive logs written, and write down this location. You should place these logs on a drive that has no redo logs assigned to it.
15. Determine where you want to store exports, and write down this location. Be sure to separate your exports from your archive logs.
16. Make a list of your initial users, along with their default applications, and note any that require the ability to create files.
17. Load the installation CD into your CD-ROM drive.
18. Log on as the *administrator* user created to own the Oracle system.
19. On NT 4.0 and Windows 2000, open the "My Computer" icon; on NT 3.51 open the File Manager.
20. Select the drive that corresponds to the CD-ROM, and double-click on *SETUP.EXE*.
21. Supply setup information. The setup executable will ask you to specify a language, a company name, and the location of the Oracle Home directory.

22. Select the installation type. You can choose any of the following from the Installation Type dialog box:

    Typical Installation
    Minimal Installation
    Custom Installation

    Using your mouse, select Typical Installation and click "OK."

23. Create your own database.

    A dialog box will appear, asking if you want documentation installed. Unless you are extremely short on disk space, go ahead and install the documentation by clicking "OK."

24. Change the default passwords. The default passwords assigned during startup are:

    - For the INTERNAL user (the ID used to start up the databases): "oracle"
    - For the SYS user: "change_on_install"
    - For the SYSTEM user: "manager"

    Change these passwords as soon as possible; if you don't, you will be leaving a significant security hole in your database.

Installing Oracle on VMS

Follow these steps to install Oracle on a VMS system:

1. Review the installation documents distributed with your software.

2. Ensure that all the requirements specified in the documentation have been met.

   Using the guides provided in the documentation, establish the proper operating system. This entails coordinating changes to the SYSGEN parameters with the system administrator and may require altering basic system user account quotas.

3. Create the Oracle DBA account.

   Prepare a detailed description of all Oracle DBA account requirements, and give it to the system administrator. (This description must include explanations of the reasons behind the quota and privilege requirements.) Have the system administrator create the required account.

4. Set quotas in the high range of those listed in the user section. In addition, the DBA account requires the following privileges:

   SYSNAM
   GRPNAM
   CHMKNL
   PRMMBX (If TCP/IP is to be used)
   GROUP
   WORLD
   ORA_DBA rights identifier

   ORA_DBA is the generic rights identifier that can access, start up, and shut down all instances. If you need finer control over who has access to what databases, use the SID in the identifier. For example, if the SID is PROD the rights identifier will be ORA_PROD_DBA. This rights identifier restricts the user to being able to start up and shut down only the PROD database. The Oracle DBA may also require the OSOPER and OSDBA identifiers.

5. Ensure that disk space and access requirements are met.

   Have the system administrator review the available disks for space availability, speed of access, and fragmentation status. If necessary, have the system administrator defragment the disks. (Defragmentation is required because Oracle prefers contiguous files.)

6. Create an installation map.

   Obtain information from the system administrator about the disks, their speeds, and their available capacities, and use this information to prepare an installation map showing file placement.

7. Create a system logical location list.

   Define a list of required system logicals to point to disk locations. The list should allow the use of wild cards to address the entire setup. For example, you might specify:

   ```
   X_ORA_DISKn
   X_ORA_DISKn+1
   X_ORA_DISKn+2
   X_ORA_DISKn+3
   X_ORA_DISKn+4
   ```

   where *X* is a site/cluster identifier and *n* is 0 or 1.

8. Define the required directory structure on each disk. The structure should start with a generic top-level directory, such as *X_ORACLE*, and have subdirectories for each instance. If you wish, you can use the Oracle convention of DB_ followed by the SID name of the database to name these directories.

   Within these subdirectories, it might be advisable to subdivide each directory into file types (if multiple file types will be stored there). Remember that if you have fewer than your optimal number of disks available, you can still assign the required number of logical disks in preparation for a time when you may have more room to spread the files. This allows you to redefine logical disks instead of entire filenames.

9. Determine how many users will be using the database, and write down this number.

10. Determine the number of redo logs, and write down this number.

11. Determine how many rollback segments you will need, and write down this number.
12. Determine the disks on which you want to place your control files, and write down these locations.
13. Determine what you want to call your instance (SID), and write down this name. The name can be up to 64 characters long.
14. Determine what you want to call your database, and write down this name. Unless you will be running multiple instances against the same database, the database name and the SID should be the same. If you are running multiple instances against the same database, append the instance number to the database name and use that for the SID.
15. Determine the size of your SGAPAD, and write down this size in kilobytes. The PAD determines how much process memory is reserved for the SGA. The default is 5120 KB, or 5 MB. We suggest that you use a minimum of 10 MB.
16. Write down the number, size, and location of the datafiles you will need.

    You will need at least five datafiles, plus two more for each application. Write down what size they should be in megabytes. Map out their locations if you have more than one data disk, and determine whether you have any large tables that might require their own tablespace areas.
17. Determine where you want your archive logs written, and write down this location.
18. Determine where you want to store exports, and write down this location.
19. Make a list of your initial users and their default applications, and note any users that require the ability to create files.

20. Copy the installation save sets to disk.

    If you have space available, have the system administrator copy the installation save sets from tape or CD onto a disk. Your access time will be decreased dramatically. Place each tape or each subsection of the CD in its own subdirectory; this is necessary because each set of files will have its own *BOOT.BCK* file. If you put the save sets in one large directory, these files will become confused and cause installation problems. If you are installing from a CD, this step is not required; however, note that disk-to-disk access is faster than CD-to-disk access.

21. Set your default directory to the top-level directory on the executable drive. The VMS command to do this is:

    ```
    SET DEFAULT disk:[directory]
    ```

    We suggest that you don't install the actual executables in a directory used as a login directory. It is best to set up a subdirectory under the top-level directory (e.g., *X_ORACLE.DBA*), and have the DBA account log in at that directory.

22. Unbundle the RDBMS save set once you are in the top-level directory by issuing the following commands:

    NOTE

    If you didn't have the disk space to unload the save sets from tape, do step a; otherwise, proceed to step b.

    ---

    a. Mount the RDBMS tape onto the tape drive:

       ```
       MOUNT/FOREIGN devicename
       ```

    b. Unbundle the *BOOT.BCK* save set:

       ```
       BACKUP/LOG devicename:BOOT.BCK/SAVE
          []*.*/NEW/OWN=PARENT
       ```

       Note that the square brackets shown here are required characters in the command.

23. Load the required products.

Use the Oracle install procedure, *ORACLEINS.COM*, to load the required products from the RDBMS save sets as follows:

a. Invoke this procedure via the following command:

```
@ORACLEINS
```

b. When ORACLEINS displays the ORACLE Installation Startup Menu, choose the first selection, "Create a new ORACLE system."

c. When you are prompted for the Oracle root directory, press Enter to accept the default value and continue. If you don't want to use the default directory, enter the location of the proper directory and press Enter.

d. When you are prompted for the location of the save sets you want to load, enter the location of the directory for the next save set if you used the preloaded save. Alternatively, enter the tape drive from which you are loading the save sets.

e. When the Main Menu appears, choose the Software Installation and Upgrade Menu.

f. When the Software Installation and Upgrade Menu appears, choose the "Select Products to Load" option.

g. When the list of applicable products from the save set is displayed, choose those you are licensed for from the menu by entering their numbers from the list. If you want to load all the products, enter an "A". To exit the menu with your selections, enter an "E". If you make a mistake, enter "Q" to exit the menu and start over.

h. When the Software Installation and Upgrade Menu is displayed, choose the "Load and Build Selected Products" menu item.

NOTE

The products will be loaded first. Then the procedure will prompt, "Do you want to re-configure the products or exit before building? (N):". Enter a "Y" unless this is the last product save set you wish to unbundle or bundle.

i. If this is not the last save set, return to step 22 and load the next *BOOT.BCK*.

j. If this is the last save set, go on by choosing "Select Build Configuration Options." Configure all products per your system requirements and then enter "E" to return to the Software Installation and Upgrade Menu. Be sure to specify the maximum PAD size you will require (from step 15) in the RDBMS Configuration Options.

k. Select the "Build Selected Products" item. We suggest that you build the OPTION item first if you are using the Transaction Processing Option (TPO), then build Net8, followed by any tools not built by the previous procedures. Note that selecting all tools to be built at once may result in products being linked multiple times.

NOTE

The OPTION product must be loaded and built if you ever intend to use TPO. If the OPTION product is not selected, it will not be built by the other build procedures.

24. Unbundle the other product save sets using steps 22 and 23. (You will have to load the *BOOT.BCK* save sets for each product from their own save set directories or tapes.) The first *BOOT.BCK* is unloaded into the top-level or root directory; all others are loaded into the install directory created when the first *BOOT.BCK* was unbundled or bundled.

25. Load all desired products before building any of them. Many of the products are dependent upon each other and will relink several times if you build the products as you load them. Use the "Load and Build" option from the ORACLEINS menu. Once the product is linked, answer "Y" when the procedure asks if you wish to reconfigure; then exit from the reconfigure menu.

26. Build the products.

    Once all products are loaded, you can begin building them. Build the following products first:

    - The RDBMS
    - Net8 (Net8 is used by virtually all the products; it will link most of them for you)
    - After the RDBMS and Net8, any tools not linked by the Net8 build

27. Create an instance.

    Once all the products have been built successfully, use ORACLEINS to create an instance by selecting the Instance Creation, Startup, and Shutdown Menu.

28. Create the database name.

    From the Instance Creation, Startup, and Shutdown Menu, select the "Create a New Instance and Database" option.

29. Enter a unique SID (the one you wrote down in step 13).

30. Enter a unique database name (the one you wrote down in step 14).

31. Check the defaults for the various system files displayed, as follows:

    a. Ensure that the redo logs are placed in the locations you chose for them.

    b. Verify that the size of the redo logs is what you need.

c. Ensure that the database (specifically, the SYSTEM tablespace) is sized for future expansion.

d. Verify that the control files are placed properly.

e. Enter the value of MAXDATAFILES (the maximum number of datafiles) from step 16, and the value of MAXLOGFILES (the maximum number of log files) from step 10.

f. Enter the value of MAXINSTANCES (the maximum number of instances that may access a single database).

g. Enter the value of MAXLOGMEMBERS (the maximum number of copies of a single log file).

h. Enter the value of MAXLOGHISTORY (the maximum number of redo logs that can be recorded in the archive history of the control file).

Once you are completely satisfied with the defaults, enter "E" to exit.

32. Begin instance setup.

The procedure builds the instance directory structure, creates database build and maintenance scripts, and creates database startup and shutdown scripts. When you are asked if you want to continue, you have two options:

a. If you don't want more than two control files and two redo logs created at this point and don't want archive logging, answer "Y" or press Return.

b. If you need to add more control files or redo logs or if you want archive logging, add this data to the creation script, answer "N", and exit the ORACLEINS procedure.

If you answered "Y", the procedure will build and start your initial instance.

33. If you chose "Y" in step 32, go on to step 35.

If you chose "N" and exited the ORACLEINS procedure, return to the Oracle root directory (using SET DEFAULT [-]) and execute a directory command (DIR).

34. Set your default directory.

    If you have returned to the root directory, set your default directory to *DB_<SID>* and then use the EDT or EVE editor to modify the *CREATE_<SID>.SQL* file so it includes the additional redo logs, control files, and archive log parameters. Once you have finished the modifications, there is a *.COM* procedure (with the same name as the *.SQL* procedure) to create your instance.

35. Add a second rollback segment.

    Once the instance is created and operational, add a second rollback segment using the procedure in the *Oracle8i Administrator's Guide* for your system. Once this second rollback segment has been created, shut down the instance and add a ROLLBACK_SEGMENTS statement to your *INIT.ORA* file with the name of the new rollback segment as its parameter. Restart the instance.

36. Change the default passwords. The default passwords assigned during startup are:

    - For the INTERNAL user (the ID used to start up the databases): "oracle"
    - For the SYS user: "change_on_install"
    - For the SYSTEM user: "manager"

    Change these passwords as soon as possible; if you don't, you will be leaving a significant security hole in your database.

37. Add any additional tablespaces you need. You can do this from SQL*Plus via the CREATE TABLESPACE command. Be sure to create a tablespace for ROLLBACK_SEGMENTS.

NOTE

For documentation purposes, to save you from having to enter the commands over and over again, and to reduce the chance of error, we suggest that you create a SQL script to create these initial tablespaces.

38. Add the necessary rollback segments.

    Using the CREATE ROLLBACK SEGMENTS command, add the rollback segments you require from step 11. (We suggest that you use simple names, such as RBK1, RBK2, RBK3, etc.) Use the TABLESPACE option of the command to be sure they are placed in the ROLLBACK tablespace. We also suggest that you create a SQL script to perform this function.

    Shut down the database. Edit the *INIT.ORA* ROLLBACK_SEGMENTS parameter to remove the rollback segment name added in step 35, and add the names of the rollback segments just created.

39. Restart the instance.

40. Drop the rollback segment from step 35 that's now offline.

    You can do this using the DROP ROLLBACK SEGMENT command. Alternatively, you can keep it for use during future maintenance of the other rollback segments.

41. Load your tools tables.

    Once the instance is created and operational, proceed with loading your tools tables. If you want the tools to reside in a tablespace other than SYSTEM, use the SQLDBA program, issue a CONNECT INTERNAL command, and then issue an ALTER USER SYSTEM command to change the default tablespace for the SYSTEM user to the desired tools tablespace. You should also use the REVOKE command to remove the global RESOURCE privilege from the SYSTEM user. Use the GRANT command to grant resources on the new default tablespace to the SYSTEM user.

42. Type `@ORACLEINS` at the command line.

    Once you're in the ORACLEINS procedure, select the "Reconfigure existing products, manage the database, or load demo tables" option from the menu.

43. Build or upgrade database tables.

    From the Oracle Product Installation and Upgrade Menu, select the Build or Upgrade Database Tables Menu. When the list of products is displayed, select the ones for which to load the tables; then exit the menu using the "E" option. The procedure will load all required tables, prompting you for any required data. Once this step is complete, the database is set up.

44. Shut down the database and take a full backup of the Oracle installation.

    This is a base installation and should be saved. Once a complete backup is taken, any archive logs accumulated during the install may be disposed of.

45. Run scripts against the SYS or SYSTEM user.

    Consult the DBA guide for any SQL scripts—for example, *UTILMON.SQL*, *CATPROC.SQL*, *CATDBASYN.SQL*, etc.—that should be run against the SYS or SYSTEM user. Once this step is complete, the database is fully operational.

46. Add users. Using the editor of your choice, create a SQL script to add the users listed in step 19. Use the following commands as a template:

    ```
    CREATE USER username IDENTIFIED BY password
    DEFAULT TABLESPACE default_tablespace_name
    TEMPORARY TABLESPACE temporary_tablespace_name
    QUOTA UNLIMITED ON default_tablespace_name
    ```

Creating a Parallel Oracle Database

Creating a parallel database starts with a single instance. This instance is created in exactly the same way as an exclusive instance. Once the first instance is up and operating, you can define the additional instances that will share the database. The final step is to synchronize the *INIT.ORA* files for the various databases and start all the instances in shared mode.

Parallel database issues

There are several parts of the database that must be considered when you're designing and starting up a parallel instance:

- File structures
- Data dictionary
- Sequence number generators
- Rollback segments
- Redo log files

By properly designing these items you can avoid resource contention, thus optimizing performance.

Instances in a parallel database have the following characteristics:

- All instances use the same control files and datafiles.
- Each instance has its own SGA and redo logs.
- Each instance can have a different number of redo logs.
- Each instance can have a different degree of mirroring.
- Each instance must have its own dedicated rollback segment(s).
- At least one rollback segment must be available for each instance. This can be guaranteed via use of private rollback segments.

Before you can start up a parallel instance, you must have sufficient redo logs and rollback segments available to split up among the instances. There must also be enough memory available on each node to handle the SGA requirements for each instance. The rollback segments can be either public or private. We suggest, though, that you make the rollback segments private so they can be positioned on the disks local to each instance and made exclusive to that instance.

You can specify additional rollback segments from any active instance. Each instance acquires whichever rollback segments you specify in the ROLLBACK_SEGMENTS parameter in its *INIT.ORA* file.

Parallel database setup checklist

Follow this checklist to make sure you are setting up the parallel database properly:

1. Create the database and the initial instance. Set the MAXINSTANCES, MAXLOGFILES, ARCHIVELOG, and MAXLOGHISTORY parameters in the *INIT.ORA* file to the proper values.
2. Modify the *INIT.ORA* parameter DB_BLOCK_SIZE to ensure that the database can provide the number of freelists and extents you will need. At this point, you should also set the DB_NAME parameter.
3. Add a second rollback segment to the database. Add the second name to the *INIT.ORA* file by modifying the ROLLBACK_SEGMENTS parameter. There is no need to shut down the instance. Once the second rollback segment is created, it can be brought online with the ALTER ROLLBACK SEGMENT command.
4. Add the required tablespaces to the instance.
5. Create additional rollback segments. There are various rules of thumb for how many rollback segments you will need. One such rule is to create one rollback segment

for every four users you expect for each instance. For example, if you expect 50 users on instance 1, 24 users on instance 2, and 50 users on instance 3, you should assign 32 rollback segments in all (including the SYSTEM rollback segment), spread over the three ORA_ROLLBACK tablespaces (one tablespace for each instance).

6. Create enough redo log threads for all the expected instances. Each thread must have at least two groups of one redo log each. We suggest that you create three groups.

7. Shut down the instance and then de-assign the rollback segment assigned in step 3 by removing it from the ROLLBACK_SEGMENTS parameter. Assign the rollback segments for this instance by placing their names in the ROLLBACK_SEGMENTS parameter.

8. Add a GC_ROLLBACK_SEGMENTS parameter to the *INIT.ORA* file, or modify the current value so it equals the total number of rollback segments ever expected to be created by all the instances in the parallel database.

   You can take the additional system rollback segment offline with the ALTER ROLLBACK SEGMENT command, and then bring on this instance's rollback segments with the same command, without shutting down the instance.

9. Add the THREAD parameter to the *INIT.ORA* file, setting the THREAD value for this instance.

10. Set the ARCHIVE_LOG_DEST and ARCHIVE_LOG_FORMAT parameters in this instance's *INIT.ORA* file.

11. Set all GC_ parameters in the *INIT.ORA* file for each instance.

12. Set the INSTANCE_NUMBER parameter in the *INIT.ORA* file for the initial instance to 1. For additional instances, increment this number so each instance has a unique value. This value determines the freelist used by the instance. If one instance uses this parameter, they should

all use it. If it is not used, each instance acquires the lowest available instance number, and you have no control over the numbers assigned.

13. Verify that the SINGLE_PROCESS parameter is set to FALSE in the *INIT.ORA* file for this instance and for all other instances in the parallel database.
14. If the instance is not already shut down, shut it down and restart it in parallel mode.
15. Create the additional instances, edit their *INIT.ORA* files, and specify the appropriate rollback segments and redo threads for each instance.
16. Create a common *INITSHARE.ORA* file, and place the common initialization parameters (those that apply to all instances) in this file. For a parallel database, all instances must have the same value for the following parameters:

    CONTROL_FILES
    DB_BLOCK_SIZE
    DB_FILES
    DB_NAME
    GC_DB_LOCKS
    GC_FILES_TO_LOCKS
    GC_LCK_PROCS
    GC_ROLLBACK_LOCKS
    GC_ROLLBACK_SEGMENTS
    GC_SAVE_ROLLBACK_LOCKS
    GC_SEGMENTS
    GC_TABLESPACES
    IFILE
    LICENSE_MAX_SESSIONS
    LICENSE_MAX_USERS
    LICENSE_SESSIONS_WARNING
    LOG_FILES
    ROW_LOCKING
    SERIALIZABLE
    SINGLE_PROCESS

Specify the IFILE parameter in the *INIT.ORA* file for each of the instances so it points to the location of the *INITSHARE.ORA* file that contains the rest of the parameters.

17. Start the additional instances in parallel.

Network Management

The third major part of an Oracle DBA's job is performing network management. Net8 is the name of the software layer Oracle supplies to enable connectivity between databases, and between databases and clients. This section is designed to help you install, configure, and test Net8 software on both server and client machines.

Net8 is configured by setting parameters in a number of configuration files, such as *tnsnames.ora* and *sqlnet.ora*. These are text files you can edit by hand, but Oracle also provides several GUI tools to make your job easier. These include:

Net8 Assistant
: A well-organized GUI interface that allows you to change virtually all Net8 parameters in all configuration files.

Net8 Configuration Assistant
: A GUI interface that runs as part of an Oracle install to help you initially configure Net8 on a system.

Easy Config
: A deprecated (i.e., soon to be obsolete) program that lets you add, modify, and delete net service names. Net8 Assistant implements the same functionality.

This list of GUI assistants is valid for Oracle8*i*. Over the years, programs have come and gone. If you are running an earlier release of Oracle, you may have a different set of utilities. You may also find it easier to edit your Net8 configuration files directly using a text editor. For details on doing that, refer to the book *Oracle Net8 Configuration and Troubleshooting* by Hugo Toledo and Jonathan Gennick (O'Reilly).

Confirming Network Availability

Before attempting to use Net8 to communicate between two computers, ensure that those two computers can communicate across the network through whatever underlying protocol you intend to use. Many of the problems users encounter when setting up distributed database solutions are the result of network, rather than Net8, difficulties.

Many of the steps in this process use the *ping* utility to test connectivity. *ping* is specific to TCP/IP network environments. If you're using another protocol, you'll need to use a utility appropriate for that protocol:

1. Use the *ping* utility in a loopback test to verify that your computer's networking software is properly configured. The standard loopback address is 127.0.0.1. Ping that, and you should get a response:

   ```
   E:\> ping 127.0.0.1
   Reply from 127.0.0.1: bytes=32 time<10ms TTL=128
   ```

   If you don't get a response from pinging the loopback address, your network software and/or hardware is not properly configured.

2. Test name resolution by issuing a *ping* command, but this time identify your computer by name rather than by number:

   ```
   ping revealnet_client01.revealnet.com
   ```

   If pinging by name fails, you have a name resolution problem. If you are using DNS for that purpose, have your system administrator check into the problem. If you are using a *hosts* file to resolve names, check that to be sure it contains entries for your computer and for the remote computer to which you want to connect. On Unix systems, *hosts* is often in the */etc* directory. On Windows NT systems, *hosts* is in *C:\WINNT\system32\drivers\etc*.

3. Use *ping* to check the client's ability to communicate with the server. If the computers cannot communicate with each other, make sure the network media, cabling, and network interface cards are connected correctly. Other possible sources of trouble in TCP/IP networks are the routers and other devices used to segment, or subnet, networks. Often, messages intended for another computer fail to reach their destination due to network segmentation problems. Contact your network administrator to correct such problems.

Confirming Net8 Connectivity

Once you have Net8 software installed on both server and client machines, it's helpful to be able to test Net8 connectivity over whatever underlying protocol you are using. Oracle supplies a utility called *tnsping* for this purpose. The *tnsping* utility is usually used to verify connectivity to a Net8 listener running on a server, but it can also be used to verify connectivity to an Oracle Names server or a Connection Manager instance.

If you have a net service name defined, you can use *tnsping* to test connectivity to the first protocol address in the net service name's address list:

```
tnsping prod_db
```

If you don't have a net service name defined, or you want to remove net service name resolution as a possible source of trouble, you can specify a protocol address directly on the command line:

```
tnsping '(ADDRESS=(PROTOCOL=TCP)
   (HOST=PROD.REVEALNET.COM)(PORT=1521))'
```

If *tnsping* fails to get a response from the remote host, you should check the following:

1. Is the remote Net8 service up and running? Usually this will be a listener, but it could also be a Connection Manager instance or an Oracle Names server. Be sure you know what it is that you are tnspinging.
2. If you supplied a net service name as an argument, does that net service name exist? Can *tnsping* resolve it?
3. If you supplied a net service name as an argument, is the protocol address for that name correct?
4. Do you have connectivity over the underlying network protocol? Go back and follow the steps outlined in the section titled "Confirming Network Availability."

NOTE

Remember that *tnsping* verifies only that you can connect to a service such as a Net8 listener, Connection Manager, or Oracle Names. A successful *tnsping* test does not indicate that the remote database is up and running.

Verifying Net8 Name Resolution

Are you trying to connect to a database using a net service name and not meeting with success? The following steps may help you troubleshoot the problem:

1. Verify the location of your Net8 configuration files. The default location on most systems is *$ORACLE_HOME/network/admin*. For Oracle8, the default location was *$ORACLE_HOME/net80/admin*. On some Unix systems, you may need to look in */var/opt/oracle* or in */etc*.

   If you have multiple copies of the configuration files in different directories, you need to confirm which set of files you are really using before proceeding.

2. Check your naming method. Look in *sqlnet.ora* for the NAMES.DIRECTORY_PATH parameter, and note the name resolution methods that are specified. You need to test each of these methods in the order in which they appear.

3. Check your default domain. Look in *sqlnet.ora* for NAMES.DEFAULT_DOMAIN. If it does not match the domain of your net service name, specify a fully-qualified net service name when you attempt to connect. Consider the following two *tnsping* commands:

   ```
   tnsping prod
   tnsping prod.revealnet.com
   ```

   If the first command fails but the second one works, you have an issue with your default domain.

   If you are using LDAP as your name resolution method, you need to look in your *ldap.ora* file and check the value of the DEFAULT_ADMIN_CONTEXT parameter. Under LDAP, the administrative context takes the place of the default domain.

4. Verify the protocol address. If you are using local name resolution, look in your *tnsnames.ora* file at the protocol address associated with the net service name. That protocol address must match a protocol address in the description list for the listener in your server's *listener.ora* file.

   If you are using Oracle Names for name resolution, you can use the Names Control utility to query the Names server for the net service name's definition. For example:

   ```
   NAMESCTL> query prod.revealnet.com a.smd
   Total response time:   0 SECONDS
   Response status:       normal, successful completion
   Authoritative answer:  yes
   Number of answers:     1
   TTL:                   1 day
   Answers:
       data type is "a.smd"
   ```

```
Syntax is ADDR:

...
(DESCRIPTION=(ADDRESS_LIST=(ADDRESS=(PROTOCOL=TCP)
(HOST=PROD.REVEALNET.COM)(PORT=1521)))
(CONNECT_DATA=(SERVICE_NAME=PROD.REVEALNET.COM)))
```

If you are using LDAP for name resolution, you can use the Net8 Assistant to verify the net service name's definition.

5. Verify that the remote listener is up and running. Connect to the remote server as the Oracle software owner, and issue the following command:

   ```
   lsnrctl STATUS LISTENER
   ```

   If your listener name is not LISTENER, replace that name with the correct listener name for your environment. On Unix systems, you can use the following command to get a list of currently running listeners:

   ```
   ps -ef | grep lsnr | more
   ```

   To see all the listeners that have been defined for a system, look at the listener address entries in your *listener.ora* file.

6. Verify that the remote database is open. Log on to the server, and connect to the database using SQL*Plus.

7. Verify that the database service is registered with the listener using the Listener Control utility's SERVICES command. For example:

   ```
   [oracle@donna /etc]$ lsnrctl services
   LSNRCTL for Linux: Version 8.1.6.0.0 - Production on
   19-JAN-2001 10:03:22
   ...
   Connecting to
   (DESCRIPTION=(ADDRESS=(PROTOCOL=IPC)(KEY=EXTPROC)))
   Services Summary...
     PLSExtProc              has 1 service handler(s)
       DEDICATED SERVER established:0 refused:0
         LOCAL SERVER
   ```

```
    prod          has 2 service handler(s)
      DEDICATED SERVER established:30 refused:0
        LOCAL SERVER
      DISPATCHER established:0 refused:0 current:0
      max:254 state:ready
        D000 <machine: prod.revealnet.com, pid: 2153>
  ...
  The command completed successfully
```

Look for your database name in the services summary. If your database is not registered with the listener, you need to look at your listener configuration and your Multi-Threaded Server (MTS) configuration.

Configuring Net8 Clients

This section details the steps involved in installing and configuring Net8 on a client system:

1. Install desired network protocols. Net8 needs to communicate over a lower-level transport protocol such as TCP/IP. Make sure you have your client configured to use the desired transport protocol prior to installing the Net8 software.
2. Install the Net8 software on your client system by running Oracle's Universal Installer from your Oracle distribution CD. A typical install will bring Net8 along with it. If you do a custom install, be sure to select Net8 Products as one of the components to install.
3. If you are installing onto a Windows system, turn off the auto-dial option from the Internet Explorer Properties window. Otherwise, your PC may attempt to dial out each time you make a Net8 connection.
4. Open your *sqlnet.ora* file in an editor, and specify Net8 name resolution methods using the NAMES.DIRECTORY_PATH parameter. For example:

   ```
   NAMES.DIRECTORY_PATH=(LDAP,TNSNAMES,ONAMES)
   ```

Note that it's possible to list more than one naming method, and that they are tried in the order in which you list them.

5. Specify a default domain using the *sqlnet.ora* file's NAMES.DEFAULT_DOMAIN parameter. For example:

```
NAMES.DEFAULT_DOMAIN=revealnet.com
```

6. If you are using LDAP for Net8 name resolution, follow the directions in the next section, "Configuring Net8 Clients to Use LDAP."
7. If you are using Oracle Names for Net8 name resolution, follow the directions in the later section "Configuring Net8 Clients to Use Oracle Names."
8. If you are using *tnsnames.ora* files for Net8 name resolution, you need to define net service names in your *tnsnames.ora* file. Either copy a standard *tnsnames.ora* file from another machine, or use the Net8 Assistant to create the net service names you need.
9. Use the *tnsping* utility to verify that you have properly established Net8 connectivity. Run *tnsping*, and specify a valid net service name as an argument.

Configuring Net8 Clients to Use LDAP

Beginning with Oracle 8.1.6, Net8 supports the use of the Lightweight Directory Access Protocol (LDAP) as a name resolution method. LDAP is now preferred over Oracle Names in cases in which you need a centralized repository for net service names.

To configure a Net8 client, do the following:

1. Specify LDAP as a name resolution method. Do this using the NAMES.DIRECTORY_PATH parameter in your *sqlnet.ora* file. For example:

```
NAMES.DIRECTORY_PATH=(LDAP)
```

2. Use the DIRECTORY_SERVER_TYPE parameter in your *ldap.ora* file to identify what brand of directory server you are using. The following example shows the proper setting for Oracle Internet Directory:

   ```
   DIRECTORY_SERVER_TYPE=OID
   ```

   Use the acronym AD for Microsoft Active Directory, and NDS for Novell Directory Services.

3. Identify an LDAP directory server on the network that the client can contact with name resolution requests. Do this using the DIRECTORY_SERVERS parameter in your *ldap.ora* file. For example:

   ```
   DIRECTORY_SERVERS=(ldap01.revealnet.com:389:636)
   ```

   The first value is the hostname of the server running the LDAP directory software. The second value is the port number to use for unsecured requests. The third value is the port number to use for Secure Socket Layer (SSL) connections.

   You can list multiple LDAP directory server addresses for the DIRECTORY_SERVERS parameter. The first address should be for your primary LDAP server, the second should be for your backup LDAP server, and so forth. Separate the addresses with commas.

4. Specify a default administrative context for unqualified net service names, using the DEFAULT_ADMIN_CONTEXT parameter in your *ldap.ora* file. For example:

   ```
   DEFAULT_ADMIN_CONTEXT="dc=revealnet, dc=com"
   ```

These steps will cause your client to use the specified LDAP directory for name resolution. You also need to ensure that you have net service names defined in that directory. Use the Net8 Assistant for that purpose. Be sure to get an LDAP username and password from your LDAP directory manager.

When you use LDAP, be aware that net service names may be specified differently in client applications such as

Oracle-supplied utilities (e.g., SQL*Plus), third-party applications, or homegrown applications. The differences come into play only when you use fully-qualified net service names.

Unqualified net service names are specified in the same manner whether LDAP is being used or not. The following example shows how you would make a SQL*Plus connection to a net service named *steve*:

```
sqlplus system/manager@steve
```

It's different when you want to specify a fully-qualified net service name. Traditionally, net service names have been organized along the lines of the Domain Name Service (DNS) used for naming Internet hosts. The fully-qualified version of *steve*, for example, might be *steve.revealnet.com*. To specify a fully-qualified net service name when you are using LDAP, use the distinguished name. For example:

```
sqlplus system/manager@"cn=steve,
   cn=OracleContext,dc=revealnet,dc=com"
```

Note that the quotes are necessary only when you enter a distinguished name on the command line. If you are filling in the Host String field for the GUI version of SQL*Plus, you don't need quotes.

Note also that `cn=OracleContext` must be explicitly specified for fully-qualified names. When you specify a complete distinguished name, Net8 won't add that component automatically, as it does when you specify a simple unqualified name.

Configuring Net8 Clients to Use Oracle Names

Oracle Names is Oracle's older centralized naming service software. Oracle Names will someday be phased out in favor of LDAP. If you have a choice of centralized naming methods, we recommend that you go with an LDAP solution if possible.

The steps needed to configure a client to use Oracle Names are not entirely consistent from one release of Oracle to the next. The process here is a reasonably "safe" method that will work for Oracle8*i* and for some earlier releases of Oracle Names (be aware that other approaches are possible, and you may see them used in the field):

1. Specify Oracle Names as a name resolution method. Do this using the NAMES.DIRECTORY_PATH parameter in your *sqlnet.ora* file. For example:

   ```
   NAMES.DIRECTORY_PATH=(ONAMES,TNSNAMES)
   ```

   With this setting, the client will first attempt name resolution using Oracle Names. If that fails, the client will fall back on local naming using the *tnsnames.ora* file.

2. Specify the protocol addresses for the Names servers you want your client to use. You can do this using the NAMES.PREFERRED_SERVERS parameter in your *sqlnet.ora* file. For example:

   ```
   NAMES.PREFERRED_SERVERS=
      (ADDRESS_LIST=
         (ADDRESS=
            (PROTOCOL=TCP)
            (HOST=names01.revealnet.com)
            (PORT=1575))
         (ADDRESS=
            (PROTOCOL=TCP)
            (HOST=names02.revealnet.com)
            (PORT=1575))
      )
   ```

When resolving a net service name, Net8 will contact each Names server in the order in which you have listed them until it finds one that resolves the name in question.

In addition to this method of specifying Names server addresses, some releases of Oracle Names support automatic discovery of Names servers on the network. When automatic discovery is used, the list of Names server addresses is written to a file named *.sdns.ora* (*sdns.ora* on Windows systems), which is located in the *$ORACLE_HOME/network/names* directory. NAMES.PREFERRED_SERVERS takes precedence over *.sdns.ora.*

Configuring Net8 on the Server

There are several options when it comes to configuring Net8 on a server, and it's impossible to detail every one of them in this book. The following process covers the tasks of installing the software and configuring a Net8 listener to handle incoming database connections:

1. Install the desired network protocols. Net8 needs to communicate over a lower-level transport protocol such as TCP/IP. Make sure you have your server configured to use the desired transport protocol prior to installing the Net8 software. Otherwise, Net8 may not install the needed protocol adaptors.
2. Install the Net8 software on your server system. Do this by running Oracle's Universal Installer from your Oracle distribution CD. You should install at least the Net8 Client and Net8 Server components. You may also want to install Oracle Names, Oracle Connection Manager, and the Oracle SNMP Agent.
3. If you expect to make client connections from your server to a remote database, you should follow the process outlined earlier in the section "Configuring Net8 Clients." Otherwise, you won't be able to use database links or do anything else that requires Net8 connectivity.
4. Locate your *listener.ora* file. It will be with all your other Net8 configuration files. The default location is *$ORACLE_HOME/network/admin.* You may need to look in */var/opt/oracle* on some Unix systems.
5. Create a listener address entry in your *listener.ora* file. This defines the protocol address, or addresses, that your listener will monitor for incoming connection

requests. The entry in the following example supports TCP/IP and IPC connections:

```
LISTENER=
   (DESCRIPTION_LIST=
      (DESCRIPTION=
         (ADDRESS=
            (PROTOCOL=TCP)
            (HOST=prod.revealnet.com)
            (PORT=1521))
      )
      (DESCRIPTION=
         (ADDRESS=(PROTOCOL=IPC)(KEY=orcl))
      )
   )
```

The part of the listener address entry to the left of the first equals sign (=) defines the listener's name. This can be confusing, because the default listener name is simply LISTENER. Be sure you understand that, in this context, LISTENER is *not* a keyword. It's a name that you can arbitrarily assign.

NOTE

The TCP/IP port number shown here is the default Net8 listener port number. If you are in doubt about what port number to use, go with 1521.

---

6. Optionally, define static services. Oracle8*i* database instances automatically register their database services with the listener. However, to support older releases of Oracle, or to support clients who connect to a specific Oracle instance using an SID, you may need to create a list of statically defined services for your listener. You can do this using the SID_LIST entry. For example:

```
SID_LIST_LISTENER=
   (SID_LIST=
      (SID_DESC=
         (GLOBAL_DBNAME=prod.revealnet.com)
```

```
            (ORACLE_HOME=/home/oracle/OraHome1)
            (SID_NAME=prod)
        )
    )
```

In this example, SID_LIST_LISTENER identifies the SID list for the listener named LISTENER. If you were defining the SID list for a listener named PRODLISTENER, you would use SID_LIST_PRODLISTENER for your parameter name. The parameters for the specific SID description shown here then go on to specify the database's global name, the Oracle Home directory, and the SID name.

7. You may also want to set various control parameters for your listener. Consult your documentation for a list of these. If you aren't sure what to do here, don't set any control parameters, and accept all the defaults instead.

8. Start your new listener. Use the Listener Control utility's START command for this purpose. The following example shows START being used to start the listener named PRODLISTENER:

```
[oracle@donna /etc]$ lsnrctl START PRODLISTENER

LSNRCTL for Linux: Version 8.1.6.0.0 - Production on
19-JAN-2001 14:07:09

(c) Copyright 1998, 1999, Oracle Corporation.  All
rights reserved.

Starting /home/oracle/OraHome1/bin/tnslsnr: please
wait...
...
Connecting to
(DESCRIPTION=(ADDRESS=(PROTOCOL=IPC)(KEY=EXTPROC)))
STATUS of the LISTENER
------------------------
Alias                     listener
Version                   TNSLSNR for Linux: Version
                          8.1.6.0.0 - Production
Start Date                19-JAN-2001 14:07:09
```

```
Uptime                       0 days 0 hr. 0 min. 0 sec
Trace Level                  off
Security                     OFF
SNMP                         OFF
Listener Parameter File      /home/oracle/OraHome1/
network/admin/listener.ora
Listener Log File            /home/oracle/OraHome1/
network/log/listener.log
Services Summary...
  PLSExtProc                 has 1 service handler(s)
The command completed successfully
```

9. Use the Listener Control utility's SERVICES command to verify that your database services are properly registered with the listener. The following example shows how to get a list of services for the listener named PRODLISTENER:

```
[oracle@donna /etc]$ lsnrctl SERVICES PRODLISTENER

LSNRCTL for Linux: Version 8.1.6.0.0 - Production on
19-JAN-2001 10:03:22
...
Connecting to
(DESCRIPTION=(ADDRESS=(PROTOCOL=IPC)(KEY=EXTPROC)))
Services Summary...
  PLSExtProc             has 1 service handler(s)
    DEDICATED SERVER established:0 refused:0
      LOCAL SERVER
  prod         has 2 service handler(s)
    DEDICATED SERVER established:30 refused:0
      LOCAL SERVER
    DISPATCHER established:0 refused:0 current:0
    max:254 state:ready
      D000 <machine: prod.revealnet.com, pid: 2153>
...
The command completed successfully
```

If you're depending on automatic registration, note that it sometimes takes a few minutes for that to occur.

10. If you want to use the Multi-Threaded Server (MTS) option, follow the procedure in the next section, "Configuring Multi-Threaded Server."

Configuring Multi-Threaded Server

Multi-Threaded Server (MTS) is a feature whereby one server process services several client connections. In a dedicated server environment, which is often what you get by default, each client connection causes a corresponding server process to be created. Having a large number of clients can drain CPU and memory resources. For applications that are not query-intensive, you can use MTS to service a large number of users with fewer resources than would be required by dedicated server processes.

MTS is configured by setting a number of parameters in your instance initialization file. You need to stop and restart your database for the changes to take effect. Be sure to allow yourself some time to fix problems, as it's not unusual for your first attempt at configuring MTS to go awry.

The process described in this section should work for any Oracle8*i* release. However, Oracle has changed MTS parameters over time, and earlier releases may require the use of parameters other than what you see here:

1. Create dispatchers for the protocols you want to support by setting the MTS_DISPATCHERS parameter:

   ```
   MTS_DISPATCHERS="(PROTOCOL=TCP)(DISPATCHERS=2)"
   MTS_DISPATCHERS="(PROTOCOL=SPX)(DISPATCHERS=1)"
   ```

   This example creates two dispatchers to support TCP/IP and one to support SPX. If you're creating multiple dispatchers for a protocol, you may want to limit the number of connections they can each handle:

   ```
   MTS_DISPATCHERS="(PROTOCOL=TCP)(DISPATCHERS=2)\
   (CONNECTIONS=100)"
   ```

You can also optionally specify a protocol address for each dispatcher, but then you must configure each one individually. Be sure each dispatcher gets a different protocol address. For example:

```
MTS_DISPATCHERS="(ADDRESS=(PARTIAL=TRUE)\
(PROTOCOL=TCP)(HOST=prod.revealnet.com)(PORT=1217))\
(DISPATCHERS=1)"

MTS_DISPATCHERS="(ADDRESS=(PARTIAL=TRUE)\
(PROTOCOL=TCP)(HOST=prod.revealnet.com)(PORT=1218))\
(DISPATCHERS=1)"
```

All MTS_DISPATCHERS parameters must be together in your database initialization file. You can put blank lines between them, but no other parameters should be specified between two MTS_DISPATCHERS settings.

2. Set the number of shared server processes you want created when you first start the instance. The following setting results in a minimum of 25 shared server processes, which will be created when the instance starts:

   ```
   MTS_SERVERS=25
   ```

3. Specify the maximum number of shared server processes to allow. The following parameter setting specifies an upper limit of 100 shared server processes:

   ```
   MTS_MAX_SERVERS=100
   ```

   Oracle will vary the number of shared server processes as demand dictates, but the number will never be allowed to drop below MTS_SERVERS, nor will it be allowed to exceed MTS_MAX_SERVERS.

4. Optionally, specify a value for the maximum number of dispatchers you will allow for an instance. You can create dispatchers dynamically while an instance is running, but only if you set the maximum number of dispatchers higher than the number you define in your

instance parameter file. The following parameter setting sets the limit at 10 dispatchers:

```
MTS_MAX_DISPATCHERS=10
```

5. If your listener isn't listening on the default TCP/IP port of 1521, you should use the LOCAL_LISTENER parameter to specify the protocol address your listener is monitoring. For example:

```
LOCAL_LISTENER="(ADDRESS_LIST=(ADDRESS=\
(PROTOCOL=TCP)(HOST=prod.revealnet.com)\
(PORT=1522)))"
```

   Defining the listener address this way is a necessary prerequisite for the instance to be able to register its database service name with the listener automatically. To register the service name, the instance needs to know how to contact the listener.

   Note that it's also possible to specify the listener address as part of the MTS_DISPATCHERS parameter. In this case, LISTENER=(ADDRESS_LIST...) is used within the MTS_DISPATCHERS parameter setting. For example:

```
MTS_DISPATCHERS="(PROTOCOL=TCP)(DISPATCHERS=2)\
(LISTENER=(ADDRESS_LIST=(ADDRESS=(PROTOCOL=TCP)\
(HOST=prod.revealnet.com)(PORT=1522))))"
```

   Once you configure your MTS parameters, you need to stop and restart the instance for your changes to take effect. You can then query the V$DISPATCHERS and V$SHARED_SERVER dynamic performance views to see the number of dispatchers and shared server processes that are running.

Tracing Client Connections

When you are faced with an intractable connectivity problem, it can sometimes be helpful to trace your Net8 connection. When you do this, Net8 writes a complete record of activity to a file, which you can review later. Use the following process to trace a Net8 client connection (all the parameters discussed here are set in the *sqlnet.ora* file on the client machine):

1. Edit *sqlnet.ora*, and specify the directory to which you want Net8 to write trace files:

   ```
   TRACE_DIRECTORY_CLIENT=e:\oracle\ora81\network\trace
   ```

   The default trace directory on Unix systems is *$ORACLE_HOME/network/trace*. On Windows-based systems, you should never set the trace directory to the root directory (*C:*, for example) of a drive. If you do so, Net8 will not write a trace file, nor will it display any error messages telling you why it did not write a trace file.

2. Specify a name for the trace file:

   ```
   TRACE_FILE_CLIENT=somename.trc
   ```

   If you want trace file names to be unique for each client connection, which is a good thing on multiuser machines, add the following setting to *sqlnet.ora*:

   ```
   TRACE_UNIQUE_CLIENT=ON
   ```

   When TRACE_UNIQUE_CLIENT=ON, Net8 will append a process ID to the name of each trace file it creates to make the names unique.

3. Specify the level of tracing you want to see. Use the TRACE_LEVEL_CLIENT parameter for this purpose. Valid values are SUPPORT, ADMIN, USER, and OFF. The following setting sets the trace level to SUPPORT:

   ```
   TRACE_LEVEL_CLIENT=SUPPORT
   ```

   SUPPORT gets you the greatest amount of trace information. ADMIN and USER get you successively less information. OFF disables the trace feature.

Once you have provided the proper trace settings in your *sqlnet.ora* file, run the application that's giving you trouble. Net8 will generate a trace file showing the details of the connection. If you set your trace level to SUPPORT, Net8 will dump copies of all packets into the trace file. This can sometimes be helpful if you need to see the specific SQL that an application is issuing.

WARNING

Be sure to disable tracing when you no longer need it by setting TRACE_LEVEL_CLIENT=OFF. Tracing incurs a high overhead and uses up a great deal of disk, so you don't want it enabled when you're not troubleshooting a problem.

Tracing the Listener

Just as it can be helpful to trace a client connection, it can also be helpful to trace the listener process. You can do that by following the steps outlined in this section. One thing to note about listener trace parameters is that they all have the listener name appended to them. Thus, if your listener is named PRODLISTENER, enable tracing by placing the following entry in your *listener.ora* file:

```
TRACE_LEVEL_PRODLISTENER=ADMIN
```

If your listener has the default name LISTENER, the parameter to enable tracing is named TRACE_LEVEL_LISTENER.

All the parameters discussed in this section are set in your *listener.ora* file. To trace a listener, do the following:

1. Specify the directory to which trace files should be written:

   ```
   TRACE_DIRECTORY_PRODLISTENER=/home/oracle
   ```

2. Specify the name you want to give your listener trace file:

   ```
   TRACE_FILE_PRODLISTENER=prodlistener.trc
   ```

3. Specify the level of trace information you want the listener to write to the trace file. Use the TRACE_LEVEL_*listener_name* parameter for this purpose. Valid values are SUPPORT, ADMIN, USER, and OFF. For example:

   ```
   TRACE_LEVEL_PRODLISTENER=ADMIN
   ```

4. If you wish, you can cause the listener to write trace information to a series of files in round-robin fashion. To do this, specify the number of files you want, and also the number of kilobytes you want the listener to write to each file before moving on to the next. The following example specifies that trace information be written to three files, with the size of each file limited to 1000 KB:

   ```
   TRACE_FILENO_PRODLISTENER=3
   TRACE_FILELEN_PRODLISTENER=1000
   ```

   You can now leave tracing on indefinitely without fear of filling your disk to capacity. You'll never have more than 3000 KB worth of trace data at any given time. You'll also have access to only the two most recently written trace files. The third file will be the one the listener is writing. As tracing switches from one file to the next, older information will eventually be overwritten. This particular feature is available only in Oracle8*i*.